Brass Tacks

Brass Tacks

"CAPSULE OPTIMISM"

by

Col. Wm. C. Hunter

Author of
"DOLLARS AND SENSE"

WILDSIDE PRESS

"BRASS TACKS" is capsule optimism.

It is truth, cheer, smiles and help.

The writer claims no strangle hold on knowledge — offers no apology. He wrote the text; the publishers believed the book would sell; it did and they will continue to print new editions as long as the people will buy.

You have the book in your hand; the text starts next page, so what's the use of wasting time trying to convince you of its worth.

BRASS TACKS is our brief.

YOU are the judge.

We rest our case.

Thanks.

BRASS TACKS

BE pleasant every morning until ten o'clock. The rest of the day will take care of itself.

MOTHER—the one person in the world whose kindness was never the preface to a request.

PICK out twelve drinking men you knew twelve years ago. Then see where they stand in the game today. That's all for the highball.

WHY is it you very seldom see a smile on a millionaire's face?

IF your object in life is nickel-chasing, you let your garden of thought grow full of weeds, and soon intellectually, you have about as much thinking substance as a flea's dream, and your ability to reason will be on a par with a monkey. Get money, but don't neglect the cultivation of the mind 'atween times.

THE trouble is many sing "We shall know each other there" in church, but they don't try to know each other here on earth.

IT'S a good plan to take your troubles to a philosophical friend who is big enough to point out the fact that you yourself are to blame for having troubles.

HERE is the history of many a rich man's daughter: She is born without a welcome, fed on a bottle, cared for by a nurse, reared in a nursery, sent away to school, dressed like a doll. She has a debut, to which eligible young men are invited, she is shown off like a horse at a horse-show and the parents are ready to receive bids for her sale. She marries, raises children, tries to raise them as she was raised, but her husband goes "broke" and she awakes to the necessity of being a mother such as her mother should have been.

GRIZZLY PETE of Frozen Dog says the "has-been" wears shiny clothes instead of shiny shoes.

WHEN we act the same in our home, whether there's company present or not, we have a pretty good stand-in with our family.

BRASS TACKS

THE ingrate, that pole cat which leaves a redolent trail. We don't like him. We hate the very tracks he leaves in the snow. He steals our good impulses. He makes us doubt the wisdom of kindness and help.

The two lowest things on the face of the earth are the ingrate and the snake's belly. This is not a spasm, but we've just run against an experience with an ingrate skunk, and we want to express our feelings and then face the light and gizzard up a bit. It takes an experience like this once in awhile to make us the better able to enjoy appreciation and thanks.

WHAT a lot of time would be saved if some of the time lost in hurrying hadn't been wasted.

DON'T tie grass in the path along which your brother travels.

A GENTLEMAN is simple and genuine. Simplicity and democracy makes him like the simple violin—at once the aristocrat of the palace and the democrat of the humble home.

DO what you are paid to do and THEN SOME. It's the THEN SOME that gets your salary raised.

EVERY "medium," every leader of a new ISM or cult or mysterious religion, makes money.

Millions chase the astrologer, necromancer, voodoo, the high priestess, the sun worshipper, the sand-eater, the fake doctor, the wonder-worker.

We don't wish to attract a shower of stones, but we regret that people won't do some good, horse-sense thinking for themselves and reject the impossible and foolish.

This fad religion and new cult business means we impoverish ourselves and enrich the teachers.

The time is coming when the false teacher will be given the kibosch, and the teacher of common sense will no longer be reviled and persecuted while alive, and respected after he is dead.

What is natural and right, is a pretty good text to start thinking on.

HERE'S a fool—the man with little money who spends it like a drunken sailor because he doesn't want others to think he has little.

OPEN that old plush-covered album and see mother's picture when she was a bride. Then think a bit.

IT'S too much to ask one to love his enemy. Let's compromise on forgetting him.

BRASS TACKS

YES, dear brother, we have been through the mill. We have had hard times and good times. We ran the gamut of human experiences.

We have had pet plans perish. We have had ideals blasted. We have lost a fortune through no fault of our own. We have been "busted," but we never acknowledged ourselves down and out.

We have learned that tomorrow is a hocus-pocus, a will o' the wisp. The thing that concerns us henceforth is today.

Save and improve your todays and your tomorrows will take care of themselves.

See here is our hand. We'll forget the mistakes and losses of the past and live today. We know how to do things better today than we did yesterday.

We are going to live today and make the day one of profit, and a lot of today deposits in the bank will make a big aggregate in the future.

WHEN you parley with wrong, you're likely to be a-goner. The man with a real gizzard gives the negative instanter.

IF you can't sing as you go along life's road, don't help the thunder to growl and drown the other fellow's singing. In other words, don't be a solemn shadow in the light of love and life.

TEN minutes at the close of each day in solitude, quietly sizing-up your actions of the day, will help a lot.

WHY is it some men who otherwise are sensible will waste time on law-suits.

THE Lord hears the prayer of the hustler who prays for work, but the man who prays for a job to be sent to him gets no results.

MANY a man courts his sweetheart in a parlor and wonders why she can't turn the trick in the culinary department.

CLASSES vs. masses. Do-ups vs. done-ups. The world is thus divided.

ANYHOW the Chinese set two good things a-rolling. First, the Golden Rule. Second, they pay their doctors only when they are well. They pay by the month and dock the doctors when their gizzards are out of whack.

IT'S easy 2 C, but hard 2 4 C.

BRASS TACKS

WE never know the real worth or hidden part of a man or melon until they are tapped.

THE path of duty is not as smooth as a railroad, but it always leads to the station of rest.

ANYWAY delusions help to make life worth living.

THOSE who spend their time trying to dress are unhappy. Those who study how to live are the happy ones.

SCIENTISTS say we get old because we precipitate lime and chemicals which harden us. We are glad to get this thing straight at last, for we always believed that we precipitated the lime and things because we were growing old.

WE have unions in everything excepting the uplift. When there is an Uplift Union, there will be fewer lawyers and jailers.

PEARY preached a latitude 90° from the following text: "Many are cold, but few are frozen."

TO earn money and pay bills seems to occupy most of a man's time, and he wonders why his home isn't happy. When he learns to earn love and pay attention to his home, happiness will ooze into his home through every crack and keyhole.

NO man with a fiery temper can accomplish much.

THERE are only two things in the world to worry over. The things you can control, and the things you can't control. Fix the first, forget the second.

UNTIL we see a man keep the money he makes at dishonest, get-rich-quick games, we'll continue to believe in the law of compensation.

TOO many of us study the wisdom of the ages gone by. The wisdom we should study is the wisdom of today.

IT never rains at Frozen Dog but Grizzly Pete says: "This is fine for ducks and dust." When it's dry for a long spell, he says: "This dry weather is fine for rheumatism."

WHEN we look at the mountains around Frozen Dog, it seems as though it would be impossible to cross the range; yet as we mount our cayuse pony and start for the hills, we find little streams along which we wend our way upward. Then there are draws, and gulches, and passes which unfold to our view as we advance slowly. We keep on our way, looking upward, and the bluff mountains open pathways to us.

By and by, we look backward and see the hills and valleys below, and we wonder as much over the hills we have passed as we do at the hills ahead.

Either forward or backward, the trail soon disappears. Yet as we go step by step, the way upward and onward shows the trail even though but a few yards at a time. We keep plugging along and finally cross the range into the next valley, and we have accomplished what the tenderfoot would call an impossibility.

Our troubles are like those hills. If we look at them en masse, we are likely to be discouraged; but if we hit the trail and look but a few rods ahead instead of a mile, we can find the trail, over, through or under the rocks, and one by one the boulders of trouble in our path will be overcome.

HAS it ever occurred to you that no one ever repeated a scandalous story with a good purpose.

NINE out of every ten rich men were poor boys. Poverty is an incentive to push. It is a well established fact that men are so constituted that they are unable to do their best work except under pressure.

It is equally true that the average man finds it extremely difficult to withstand the enervating effect of prosperity.

Place your son above the possibility of want and you remove the greatest source of inspiration from his life.

The men who have figured most prominently on history's pages owed their success largely to the fact that they were poor, and did not want to remain in poverty. So, brethren, if you are poor, remember you have an advantage; for wealth is a handicap to effort.

YOU may lead a fool to talk, but you can't make him think.

MANY men save up their pennies, and their dollars are blown in by their heirs.

WE have never delved into ancient history, but our opinion off-hand is that the owl was used as a symbol of wisdom, because he never expresses his thoughts in words.

AN evil thought does little harm, if you don't express it to listening ears.

IT'S hard to convince a guinea hen she doesn't know as much about music as a mocking bird. There are a lot of human guinea hens.

THE universities turn out men with cap and gown who feel they are superior beings, ready to start way up high in the ladder of fame and action.

Most of these men get a jolt and find that they have learned much of classics and of figures, but that they are shy on the great asset—experience.

Now, old experience shows one thing you can't dodge, and that is: A plan fundamentally wrong, like a building out of plumb, will fall. It's our old friend, the law of compensation.

You and I work hard; we have patience; progress seems slow. We get envious of our fellows who seem to be going forward by leaps and bounds. Don't worry, brother. Old compensation says, "You can't go fast far."

Cheer up. Be bright. Do right. Get in a business that is right and honorable, and don't worry over the seeming success of the fellow who has the "get-rich-quick" game, for tomorrow he will get poor quick, says old compensation.

WHEN you make your will, put nothing but tenderness, kindness and consideration into it.

Your will is to be read after your funeral and it is a message from the dead.

All your hate should be interred with your bones—let love alone live.

Bronze compliments, embossed deep on a tombstone, never yet thrilled human hearts like loving words in a will.

※ ※

THE average American business man cusses the waiter, because he is in a hurry and the dinner is delayed. After he has eaten, he lights a cigar and then tells funny stories and wastes twice as much time as he had to wait for his meal.

※ ※

WHEN in doubt, lead a trump. This refers to business as well as cards.

※ ※

YES, brethren, it will be proper to speak to one another in heaven without an introduction.

※ ※

ONE must be in business with a man to know him, and in love with a woman to know her, and even then they will likely keep you guessing.

THE doctors tell us that nervous prostration is generally found among women who haven't anything to do. They tell us that the mother of children who is busy with her housework seldom gets the ailment. Wouldn't it seem wise, therefore, ye women who idle and "shop," for you to get busy and chase Old Worry out of the home.

CHARACTER is found in the torrents of life. He who listlessly drifts with the tide, yielding to every appetite or passion, will very soon dash, a broken wreck, on the sullen, fagged rocks that lurk unseen in the river of life.

Happy is he who is so constituted that with a steady eye on the compass, a strong hand on the tiller, reinforced by a determined will, he guides his craft past the hidden dangers, and finally anchors safely in some quiet harbor in a position to enjoy with his loved ones the fruit of the struggle; and at last, when the supreme moment arrives calmly goes to his eternal rest, content in the thought that he leaves to posterity an unsullied name, and that the world is a gainer because of his having lived.

IN the good old days of American statesmanship, some of our United States senators were famous; today some of them are notorious.

MONEY isn't in it. When will people learn this? When will they believe it? When will they quit chasing material and seek mental pleasures?

The old man tells us—and he has experience—that all you get out of life is board, clothes, love and happiness, and that money alone, can only buy board and clothes.

RIGHT will win from the objective of happiness and peace.

Mystery is a cloak many use to make their operations seem wonderful, but the time is here when simple, old-fashioned honesty is being used as the best policy; not through conviction that honesty is right, but because it really is the best policy.

Show your hand, tell the truth, hustle and put yourself into your business and you will succeed in the measure that yourself deserves success.

SILENCE is sometimes as eloquent as a thunderbolt; as for instance when your mother-in-law looks at you, but speaketh not.

THE old maid has one important use in the world. She makes her married sister see how happy is the home where there are children.

MONEY doesn't really make the mare go, but it certainly is an inducement to incidental effort.

WEBB GRUBB says that a woman in politics is like a rose in a mud puddle.

THE prodigal son is the young man who loses everything excepting his way home.

IT'S surprising how well a homely man looks in a picture.

POOR boy, rich man. Rich son, poor grandson. That's the way the world evens up things.

HOW fine it would be if we had less law, less lawyers, and more living and more lovers.

THE fool eats and drinks too much. His stomach gets out of whack, then he criticises everybody and everything. He grumbles and does not know it's his own folly that causes people to hate him.

WE'RE sorry for the woman who is attacked by scandal; whose name is dragged down by the hyenas. It's a nasty business, and circulating malicious lies about a woman ranks with grave robbing and other peculiarities of the vile and degenerate.

Man's first care should be to shield and protect a woman's name. When he traduces, he proves himself a cowardly cad and a hound pup, and he should be tin-canned and kicked out of the atmosphere of men who remember they have wives, mothers and sisters.

BRASS TACKS is of and for Today. Yesterday is gone. We cannot change what happend then. Our concern is to live each day in act and thought and word, so we may have peace and happiness as we go along the road.

We say a great deal about Today and we do it purposely; and for fear some of our friends may get a wrong twist on this Today business, we will make the point clear.

We do not mean "Eat, Drink and Be Merry, for tomorrow ye die." That isn't our understanding of the Today idea.

We know that the kind word, helping hand, gentleness, and doing good brings joy. We know you can't change any act of yesterday. We may not be here tomorrow. We are here TODAY and the time to do things is NOW.

We have problems and tasks which we can never finish Today. Yes, indeedy! but if we get busy and tackle one thing at a time, and get that down and hog-tied, we can tackle the next thing; and one thing at a time well done, eats into a pile of things waiting for us to do.

The ox-team moves slowly. But the ox-teams took the Forty-niner from the Missouri to the Pacific. Each day the oxen did their best. Each day was a link in a mighty long chain. Each day was Progress.

If we spend Today in struggle and ambition and selfishness, we have spoiled it and it passes into a yesterday, the looking back to which gives us no pleasure.

There are pleasures and occupations and duties for each day of our lives, and we must do things Today which are of Today.

WHY worry about what to give for Christmas presents. Buy nut picks. Those in the pink satin boxes. The style never changes; the nut picks are never used; the silver plating therefore never wears off, and the nut picks and case will be a monument to the generosity of the giver that will endure forever.

IT'S better to tell the truth and run, than to lie and get caught in the act.

"THE worst of it is, you tell the truth" was the statement one of our critics made. That's just it. Sometimes the truth makes our readers squirm and they write to criticise us. We're too busy to notice it.

We know that dogs bark at the moon; but the moon doesn't answer. Happily, however, our letters generally are full of encouragement. We get just enough roasts to make us the more vehement in handing out plain, unvarnished truth.

❧ ❧

A YOUNG man chided his bride wife, that she couldn't make bread like his mother made, and she reminded her husband in return that he couldn't make the dough like her father used to make.

❧ ❧

SOME day a bright philosopher will make a hit writing good things about "father."

Mother has always had a monopoly on praise and father has always come in for a roast.

❧ ❧

HAVE you ever considered how contemptible a thing it is to invent lies about a person you don't like?

If you make a mistake and offend a friend, don't hesitate to apologize. It will make you bigger, broader, happier, and will prove you as a man instead of a sham.

WHEN hate strikes a blow, the hater's arm is likely to be fractured by the act.

GRIZZLY PETE says, "In the daytime I'm too busy to worry and at night I'm too sleepy."

MALICIOUS innuendo and ridicule are cowards' weapons

IF we were all satisfied, we would never reach the hill-tops.

THE young man thinks the Swiss apron with the ribbons and lace makes his intended look like a picture, as she presides at the chafing dish; but after he puts the ring on her finger and planks down the five to the preacher, he sighs because she hasn't a pin-checked blue gingham and can't preside gracefully over the cook stove.

WHEN the boy with his first job tells his mother he is doing the real work at the office, and that his boss is getting the credit, that is the time to play a tattoo on the rotunda of the boy's jeans to bring him to his senses.

ADVICE is asked merely to have your opinion confirmed. If the advisor differs from your views, you say he is prejudiced.

WHEN a youth is eighteen, he is in love with a girl of thirty-six. When he's thirty-six, his eyes are on the girl of eighteen.

YOU can get much advice from your maiden aunt on the rearing and caring of children.

BE not discouraged, brethren, the future will be better. Even now we are beginning to see hope in the near future. Yes, it really does look as though we can finish battleships and public buildings before it's time to discard them as useless.

THE greatest problem Percy has at his counter is to guess whether a woman is a buyer or a shopper.

USUALLY the corned-beef husband has a bric-a-brac wife.

MANY women cling to their sweetheart's neck, but after marriage they perambulate on the aforesaid neck.

A WOMAN tells fairy stories to her children to quiet them. A man tells fairy stories to his wife for the same reason.

IN the nature of things, it is well that woman was the very last work of creation; otherwise, she would have insisted on bossing the job.

NOTHING is more than half as good as it would be, if it was twice as good as it is. On the other hand, everything is twice as good as it would be, if it were only half as good as it is. The viewpoint determines whether you are a pessimist or an optimist.

WE knew a man who worked his way from poverty to riches and lived to good, happy old age, and he always minded his own business.

A MAN may get his foolish traits from his father, but names like J. St. Clair Jones are usually given by mamma.

MANY women would spend less time watching their husband's morals, if they paid more attention to his meals.

WHEN your wife asks you, "Who is the prettiest woman in this ball-room?" don't rubber around the room.

IF everything everybody wished would happen, what a mess there would be in this world.

FATE is really very kind; every worthless man gets along far better than he deserves.

MUCH of the discomfort in this world is caused by people neglecting their business to lie about each other.

MANY who "cast their bread upon the waters" expect club sandwiches to be returned to them.

DOES the word "Hock" on wine labels, or when used as a toast, mean that the more you drink, the more likely you will be to have to hock your watch?

A WOMAN whose husband is poor has at least the satisfaction of knowing he is not attractive to other women, but is all hers.

THOU foolish, gold-blinded man. Thou spendest thy Health getting Wealth, then thou wakest up and hast a pain, and the doctor looks wise and thenceforth thou spendest Wealth getting Health. What about the future you dreamed of and worked for, while you forgot Today?

If you had lived successive days, you would have been well and happy all your life. Young man, heed this, and profit by the experience of the fool. Spend your days keeping health instead of spending your health getting wealth.

A SHORT time ago, as we were sitting on our veranda in Frozen Dog Ranch, just smokin' and thinkin', Grizzly said: "Colonel, them violets are pretty in this valley, but old Webb Grubb don't see 'em for he's always looking over to see the golden rods growin' on the butte."

"That means there's happiness all around us, but we're generally lookin' way over yonder at the hills and forgettin' the valleys where we are."

A GOOD man doesn't often blow his own horn, because he's too poor to own one.

A FAST horse can't go fast far.

MANY people dance when the devil plays the fiddle, and they won't stop until the floor catches fire.

NO lie can hurt a man for a long time. There is little use in spending your time trying to correct lies. The lie itself will drop like a feeble shaft against the armor of truth.

The thing for us to do is to so live and so act the truth that a lie will not obtain. Lies do not hurt; it is the truth that hurts, and it behooves us to see that there are no weak spots in our lives where our names may be attacked truthfully.

There is nothing that will choke off lies and cause them to wither and die like supreme indifference.

Time is a great leveller, and if we have gizzard enough to act the truth and to maintain silence about lies, the lies will die and be forgotten.

MANY men figure just how far they dare to be bad.

MONEY talks, but not in the presence of the man who has wisdom.

MAKING money and making love are alike, in that the more you get the more you want.

THE man with red hair must be careful that his words and actions are not of the same warm hue.

THE man with one idea is sometimes a bore; sometimes an inspiration. It depends on the man and the idea.

MANY a life has been wasted by parents preferences and false estimates of the child's talents.

IN order to rid ourselves of dry, lonesome montony, it is necessary to have a personality and let it assert itself.

SOCIETY—we have much in our minds to say of it; but we don't want to nourish the pessimism in us, so we will drop the question.

MISFORTUNE is a great breeder of graft and dishonesty.

AN umbrella will keep the sun off all right, but you can't make much of a living holding an umbrella in one hand and working with the other.

MOST generally you can't tell what's inside of a man by what you can see on the outside. You can't hide truth very long.

WHEN looking at ourselves, we call it firmness. When looking at others, we call it stubbornness and meanness.

THE more a man finds fault, the more proof that he hasn't done anything worth while himself.

REMEMBER in business that success depends on the man and not on the plan.

NOTWITHSTANDING it's the most talked of, most roasted thing in the world, we still have weather.

AN honest man has a chance to succeed, but a dishonest man has no chance whatever.

IF you take one man's advice, the chances are the next man who comes along will convince you the first man was wrong.

IT does seem, brethren, that when you are on your way to deposit some money in your savings account, you always meet some one on the road who puts up a mighty strong appeal for that money.

THE house-fly. The common, annoying, tickling, buzzing house-fly is like the idler who bothers you. The fly hastens thither from the pot which boileth and comes not hither while the pot sizzles. Likewise the idler cometh not hither if ye are busy and thy pot boileth with thy duties.

FEAR makes pygmies. Gizzard makes giants.

THERE is a big difference between imitating a good man and counterfeiting him.

FLATTERY—the art of making others believe you are interested in them when in reality they make you weary.

THE man who wears side whiskers is either a philanthropist or a fake. No half-way man indulges in side whiskers.

A MULATTO porter chided a coal-black porter thusly: "What makes you so black, Sam?" and the reply was: "My mother was a lady."

❧ ❧

THE author's crest has these words on the scroll: "Dum Spiro Spero," which means, "While I live I hope," or words to that effect. Thank you, bright ancestor of ages ago. The motto has been an inspiration to the author and a very present help in time of trouble.

❧ ❧

TO our friends who criticise this book, we will relieve our minds by admitting our talks are full of breaks and mistakes.

The man in Texas said, "Where are we at?" The college professors were jarred at the expression, but the rank and file understood.

The big friend who helps us is not to be questioned as to how he dresses or combs his hair.

All we are after is to tone up your gizzard.

The medicine may not look well or taste good, but if it does the work, our aim is accomplished.

We need pebbles and glass and grit in a gizzard anyway. It helps digest the good stuff.

Get all the good you can out of these lines, and roast the balance to your heart's content. We haven't time to answer. We're too busy.

"DON'T do nothin' too much" is a favorite saying of Grizzly Pete of Frozen Dog.

WHEN a man gives you his reason for an act, just remember the chances are, nine times out of ten, the reason is a trail blinder.

NOW let heartless critics rail, and the pitiless world rail; but nevertheless, here's our heart's thought: He who hath power in this world, like a governor or a captain of industry, and doth not temper justice with mercy, will cry himself blind at the judgment throne for the mercy he withheld from others while here on earth.

The penitentiaries are full of men who would be free if mercy were in the gizzard of the pitiless prosecutor, whose only object is to convict.

MANY a young man is called "fast" by his friends, but "slow" by his tailor.

IF you cannot shout happiness songs from the hilltops, you can say Amen in your little valley where you are.

WHEN you came into the world, you had a birthright one talent. Shakespeare wrote plays; Raphael painted a Madonna; Newton discovered gravity; Edison made electricity obey him. These men found their talents.

Have you found yours?

WE gizzardites are a rich lot. We have health, strength, love and friendship. We strive to change sick hearts into strong gizzards. We live today and we preach that gospel to our brothers.

We hum songs of joy. We smile as we pass along. We help solve riddles for the weak and weary ones in shadowland.

We may be knocked down once in awhile, but we are up and at it before the referee counts us out.

We pass this doctrine to those who need it and the act pays us back in happiness.

THERE are enough written good things in the world to fill the Congressional Library, but most of it is old and musty, and we fall asleep as we read it. Somehow many of the old truths haven't the right hook on them.

There is nothing new, from the standpoint of thought. All that's new in these lines is the manner of serving. We talk the language of today.

THE man who gets angry suffers more than the fellow who is the object of his anger.

THE gizzardite says, "I am here. I will live today. I have a gizzard and I am not down and out until my breath stops and my heart is motionless."

EVERY man who has saved $1,000 is thereafter a safe and conservative man.

WE like to be laughed at for our wit, but not for our folly.

IT'S no satisfaction to have a lemon presented to us with a beautiful line of conversation. Usually the smoother the gab, the smoother the dose, and you don't wake up until you have swallowed it. Watch out for the smooth man with the high-falutin' language.

WRITTEN on most men's brows is "I Will." In games, pleasures, business, love or research, men strive to be it. They jostle the weak. They chill sentiment, drown sympathy, kill the finer things in life, just to be "IT." And generally, when you are it, what of it?

THE "sights" of youth are generally sight drafts, payable when you are forty or fifty years old, and Gee whillikens what interest you have to pay.

※ ※

WE haven't much time to waste on the fellow who was born with gold teeth and a silver spoon in his mouth. Such people never have felt and never will feel the deep tones and high notes we've listened to. They have drifted along; everything planned for them; no initiative necessary. They don't know it, but we have them skinned when it comes to life.

We've been through the mill of hard knocks, you and I, haven't we? We've groped in shadowland; we've basked in sunshine.

We've heard the call of the poor and weary ones who were ready to lay down, and we've helped them to help themselves.

We've had experience; aye, and much more than most folks; and what we write, we have felt.

※ ※

DON'T hope for the best, but hop for it.

※ ※

THE red sled you gave your first boy on Christmas, when you were poor, gave you more pleasure than the dress suit you bought him in after years when you were rich.

WE never saw but one honest horse race and the fellow on the leading horse had stolen it.

ONCE in awhile a woman in this great world walks off the dock in the darkness, and struggles for life in the deep waters.

Society leisurely picks up a coil of rope, but before throwing it, demands of the drowning one a certificate of character from her pastor or a letter from her Sunday school superintendent.

Not being able to produce these, the struggler is left to go down to her death in the darkness.

If we are out to save souls, why do we discriminate between the "good" and "bad?" Why is this?

THE little fish is the sweetest, and the simple joys of life leave a sweet taste on the conscience.

THE gobbler doesn't spread his tail feathers when his head is falling on the block.

UNTIL we see a rich young woman marry a poor old man, or a poor old woman marry a rich young man, we'll continue to disbelieve there's real love in the June and December marriages.

THE man and the cucumber are valueless when they are ripe.

THE most successful liar is the one who lies the least.

WHEN an ostrich or an eagle dies, its mate never marries again; and yet men have selected that nocturnal prowler, the owl, as the emblem of wisdom.

LOVED one! Just remember today is the day you worried about yesterday and the day before yesterday; and today isn't what you expected. Now this is truth from my heart to thine—the thing you are worrying about will not happen tomorrow. So cheer up and live today.

THE Sunday school teacher asked the bad boy if he knew the difference between the Universalist and Methodist? To which he replied, "There's a h——l of a difference."

WHEN you know a man is a liar, you need fear him not. For a liar is, has been, and will always be a coward.

BRASS TACKS

A COQUETTE is a rose from which every lover picks a leaf and the thorns are left for the husband.

❧ ❧

THE thin man ever hovers around the ladies. He is active, quick, and the creases in his clothes remain a long time. The thin man is always used by the tailors for the fashion plates.

Yon fat man hath a tranquil look. He is slow to move. His coat is not like the fashion plate, and verily his trousers bag at the knees; but he hath money in the bank. He owns a home, and after he passes over the Divide, along comes his thin heirs and blow in his estate.

❧ ❧

THE finer the teeth, the oftener and the wider the grin.

❧ ❧

YOU have a certain thing you can do well. So have we; so has every one. The whole problem is to get your talents in the right groove, where they will fit What we call failure is merely misfit.

Remember failure is simply a plan gone to wreck. Remember it's always the man and not the plan we should look at.

If you have plans which have gone wrong, try another and another, until you get the plan that fits you—the man.

WE have a firm conviction and well-founded belief that Morals, Anarchists and horse-thieves should be elevated.

YOU have seen the thin-faced, narrow-chested, lavendar-shirted, receding-chinned young man in the wash-room of a Pullman. He smokes a doped cigarette before he dresses, or eats his breakfast. Poor fellow! He gets his punishment right here on earth and there's no need of our deploring the scarcity of denunciatory adjectives to express our opinion of him.

Poor little gimlet-head! How we wish he had a gizzard and a brain.

THERE'S one little satisfaction when a man falls sick, it makes his wife repent of her ill treatment of him. Don't work the game too often, however.

WE pay too much attention to the material—the physical. We say a man failed. The fact is his business failed. The man didn't. The man is alive and he has experience.

Only three or four per cent of men succeed in business. That is, make it pay. So if your business doesn't go, you have a great host in the same boat.

If your plans go wrong it is because you couldn't get enough YOU in the plan.

WHEN you spend half your time making promises, you'll find it takes the other half to make excuses.

LIFE has three periods. The prospective youth. The Now of middle age and the Then of old age.

The man who skins others, turns sharp corners, jostles the weak and is suspicious during the Now period, has little satisfaction in looking backward in his old age.

One of the great pleasures of our latter days will be retrospection. Hence the importance of doing and acting things today that will give us pleasure to look back to on the morrow.

Yesterday is gone. We can't change it. But today is here. Let's improve it and put pleasant things in our bank of life that we may draw upon in after years.

HE who gets rich quickly usually gets poor quickly.

DELIVER us from indifference.

WE'VE come to the conclusion that if you make a mistake it's better to acknowledge the corn than to lie out of it.

A LITTLE word in kindness spoken,
A motion, or a tear, has often
Healed the heart that's broken
And made a friend sincere."

MONEY—the chase for which makes greed, selfishness and stagnant integrity. Money with many is the ark of the American Covenant. It has been made to mean so much socially and politically.

Money is bowed down to. Men who have it are followed and obeyed, and they generally get the grand kowtow and oriental salaam. Yet we are not discouraged, for on the horizon of the future, we see honor, virtue and love. Three bright stars of hope; and after we are satiated with this money worship, we'll turn to the brighter and better things.

We are slaves to money. The Eastern man is peculiarly the dollar serf. The West yet has more independence, and there we are planting original, simple Americanism. The West and the East are flesh brothers, but one has the shackles and some day the Western brother will free the brother of the East. Men in the West will scratch the soil, raise enough for themselves, and when the East asks for bread, the West will hold the whip handle.

EVERY big business starts in an attic, or a cellar.

THE man with a gizzard feels his pulse-beats say: "Go-go-go."

MEN will promise women and babies anything to keep them quiet.

MATERIAL pleasures are often the flush and joy of a day, and the headaches and paleness the day after.

WEBB GRUBB, the meanest man in Frozen Dog, says, "The reason the church socials do not have prettier girls is that the real pretty girls of the church are discovered by the dancing element and kidnapped."

A GOOD pilot is rather to be chosen than a great quantities of life preservers.

EGO-ISM looks through the small end of the telescope. Egotism looks at you through the big end.

MARK this, you man who has done wrong—that peculiar look in your wife's eye when she smiles at you means revenge.

A KNOWLEDGE of how to make a living is better than four diplomas in dead languages.

LETS get at things straight from the shoulder. Say what you mean.

Chuck the hothouse myopic views of life and strange, hysteric vagaries.

Rhetoric, spelling, punctuation, faultlessness of style, are all right if the thing you are trying to say is all right.

Too many attempt to portray things they don't know about, and they conceal their ignorance midst a wilderness of words and an array of glittering generalities.

Verbosity is like bird shot. Brevity is like a bullet.

ONE woman sits and sighs about her wrongs, and another storms and raves about her rights.

WHEN joy plays the fiddle, trouble can't keep from dancing.

WORSE than the thief is the ingrate, for he is a thief who steals our goodness and kindness, then stabs you, then twists the dagger.

LIVE today, preach and practice the science of making each day a profitable day. Cultivate force Eliminate wrong and all unpleasant things. Look upon today as your day and remember each moment is precious.

Get in tune with goodness. Dodge discord. Pass some word of cheer to the discouraged who are in shadowland.

If you suffer pain, remember yesterday's pain is gone, and tomorrow's pain will never come.

Heads up, brothers. Brace your backbone and forget your wishbone.

The Great World is for us. The all-seeing, all-knowing, all-powerful Being who made Today made it a Good Day. Here and there are clouds, but above the clouds the sun smiles upon us.

Remember, we are as our thoughts are, and thinking goes on all the time. If we let our thoughts run to material and physical things all the time, we are on the wrong track. If we think and act right and train our thoughts on the great and good things, we get great results.

Brothers, Today is ours! Let us improve it.

VERILY, we men have problems to solve that would test a Solomon. If your wife is sick and you say she looks badly, you have no tact. If you don't notice she is sick, you are a heartless brute.

WE haven't much patience with the fault-finder. Life is short and Today is our principal concern. Do right Today and repeat every twenty-four hours, and you'll find tomorrows will take care of themselves.

Get mental ideals, not material ideals.

Whenever a fellow is doing his best, clap him on the back and say, "Good for you."

There are too many pessimists in the world telling you unpleasant things. Don't help their game.

Smile, anyway!

OH, you West! Oh, you Idaho! Oh you Frozen Dog! The wheels of time have turned. It seems but yesterday when we were tramping the mountains of Frozen Dog.

We saw those granite hills carrying millions of tons of snow.

We saw the sage-brush valleys and we heard the call of the West.

The hills and sun-kissed valleys beckoned and we responded.

The desert has blossomed as a rose and Frozen Dog Ranch we dreamed of years ago is now a reality.

As we sit on the veranda of our Frozen Dog ranch-house and watch the lavendars, and blues, and pinks of the sunset on Seven Devils mountains, we muse, "What time hath wrought."

BRASS TACKS

We read by electric light from the power furnished by those hills. Hot and cold water faucets are in the house. Fountains in the yard. Flowers, roses, fruit trees, alfalfa have superseded the sage-brush.

We breathe the air of freedom and we live Today. The coyote howls over yonder in Freeze Out Pass. The woodchuck whistles from his den in Frozen Dog butte, just to remind us of yesterday as we first knew it. Frozen Dog, the butt of the cartoonist, is now the admiration of the people in the beautiful Payette Valley.

Grizzly Pete's check is good at the bank and his word is good anywhere in Idaho; and so, as Grizzly Pete says, "I found myself a-figgerin' if Rockafeller and Wall Street was arrayed 'gainst old Joe Kip and Frozen Dog, well, you bet, I wouldn't trade."

Brothers, when your hairs are turning gray, and your heart is sad and heavy, come out to Frozen Dog and breathe the medicin' of the hills, and get new red blood in your veins and tone up your gizzard.

YOU can get along mighty well with a fellow who hates the same man you hate.

MANY a woman wants her husband to become famous so she can snub certain other women she has a grudge against.

OF all the wild oats sown, none are used for breakfast food.

THREE wonderful things will happen some day, brethren:

1st. We will see all men rather earn an honest living than hold a political job.

2nd. We will see a hot and cold faucet in a sleeping car that knows how to differentiate.

3rd. We'll see country people who can accurately tell the number of miles it is to town.

GRIZZLY PETE and his wife went to see the President recently. We asked Mrs. Pete how she liked the looks of the President? She replied she "hadn't seen much of him, as she was spending her time looking at Grizzly and noticing how much better and nobler looking he was than the President."

Such women are the ones who get silk dress patterns from their husbands.

THERE are two words in the English language, simple words in themselves, yet they have caused untold misery. They have broken friendship, disrupted homes, broken hearts, and killed people. Those words are, "They say."

REVENGE. That's the poorest compensation man ever worked for, and court dockets and law-suits show up more mean natures than we believed could exist.

What profit is it to win a dinky law suit and get judgment for a pittance when you've paid big bills to the lawyers, and big drafts on your nervous system.

Revenge for the putty-brained man and not for the gizzardite, who is too busy to spend time on "such-a-foolishness" as revenge.

THERE is one satisfaction comes from the recent depression. We hit the bottom. We are now on the climb and good times are ahead of us. Now it is up to us to profit by our past experience. Let's not do a dollar's business on six cents. Let's swallow what we chew before we take another bite.

NEVER judge a man by the clothes he wears, for many a patched pair of trousers covers an honest heart.

HERE'S a problem we would like the answer to: Is the tip we give the waiter a bribe for him to give you something you are not entitled to, or is it a blackmail to keep him from insulting you for receiving your order?

WE'RE trying to find the good streaks in things. A mine is a dirty place. The ore is not beautiful, but the gold is there. There's lots of things in our lives that look forbidding, but the good is there. Let's find it. Smiles beat frowns. The cynic and the pessimist come nearest happiness when they are miserable.

Life is short. We have a few Todays we know about. The tomorrows are speculation, but if our Todays are all right, we get the habit, and when tomorrow is Today, we'll know how to make the best of it and get the good there is in it.

We haven't much patience with the long-haired, wise boys who lay out a line of thought and claim to have solved the riddles.

Each of us must do the thing ourselves. We must think with our own brains and listen to others, but accept no man's philosophy as our rule and guide. There are a billion brains in the world, all different. There are certain rhythms and notes of harmony, however, we all can feel and respond to.

When a man does his best each day, his record sheet is marked a 100.

Your best may be better than our best, but best is superlative from the standpoint of the individual and he gets the hundred mark, no matter whether the best is great or small.

We'll say, hurray! for your best opinion, and for Bill Jones's and Mother Eddy, and everyone who starts people thinking. We can't think your way or their ways, but anyway you and they start the ball of thought a-going, and thought much indulged in by a fair man finally gets the bull's-eye.

You may be above, and we may be below the black spot in the target, but as long as we shoot at the target of truth, we get nearer and nearer the center.

Just do the best you can Today and you are on the right track.

GRIEF starts on the surface, but when it bores into the soul, it's agony.

ONE Keeley runs a brewery; another Keeley a jag cure. It's a fight all the time. A tug-of-war, this road we travel, and the crowd is pulling both ways all the time.

SOMEHOW we never could believe political stories floated to us on a whiskey breath.

START a new religion. Make it a cross between theosophy and moonshine. Make it something you can't explain, and you will have converts galore.

Talk and preach old-fashioned horse-sense, kindness, love, and simplicity, and only the few will listen.

Living today, one day at a time, but really living, is the thing. You can't preach it, but some day you'll have it and then you'll understand.

WE can all obtain the things which are necessary and good for us, but it is the chase for possession of things which are not necessary and not good for us that makes unhappiness. Gilt-edged stocks don't make gilt-edged thoughts, a city mansion, a country home, the seductions of society, the pursuit of the aniseed bag will not make up for the dearth of contentment. Cut out superfluities; begin to live today. Learn the simple things, the kind word, the helping hand, the cheery presence, the smile. These are the jewels you should seek.

The old-fashioned rose on the dining table of the simple home brings more satisfaction than the orchid in the conservatory.

LIGHTNING doesn't strike twice in the same spot, but it's nevertheless good practice to steer clear of the locality where it's been in the habit of hitting.

THE meanest trick is to unjustly abuse a worthy man.

ANYWAY those who boast loudest of their ancestry don't live up to standard of their ancestors.

MANY a time we start out in the morning with good resolutions, and by noon-time we're limping a bit.

BRASS TACKS [55

OUR ancestors had faith. Their descendants have fakes.

AN old man told us recently that the best luck came when he was behaving best.

YOU don't have to go to perdition because people talk about you.

WHAT have you done this day in the way of showing kindness, appreciation and love?

IF the editor makes a mistake, he has to apologize. When the doctor makes a mistake, he buries it.

The doctor uses words a foot long. When the editor does it, he is criticized. The doctor goes to see another man's wife and charges the man. When the editor does this, he gets a charge of buckshot. Verily, the editor hath his trials!

FIGURES won't lie, but liars can and will figure.

THE front door of the business man's office says "push". The front door on the city hall says "pull."

NOTHING equals the scorn of a hard-working woman when you suggest Physical Culture to her.

MOST girls are more proficient in handling a curling iron than a potato peeler.

MAN hears mighty few kind words. He doesn't suit his wife or his children. The neighbors criticise. Man hears so few kind words that when they do come he will almost shrink as from a blow.

WHEN a man gets down, he is like a steer or a wolf. His fellows pounce on him.

THE remark of a fool often discounts the unspoken thoughts of a wise man.

SORROW ever knocks at our door, but if Joy is playing the fiddle she won't come in.

THE poor man dances the double shuffle glad he is alive. The rich man has the rheumatism because he doesn't exercise.

GOOD results always follow honest earnest persistent effort.

WHEN your friend looks at the wall when you are telling him your troubles, or asking him a favor, it's time to grab your hat and get out, for you are wasting time.

WHY is it that when the reformer is searched we find a knife up his sleeve.

A HORSE that has run away and a man who has shone in society never amount to much thereafter.

WE walked down State Street the other afternoon and never again will we doubt woman's courage. The costumes some of them wore testified to their bravery.

A WOMAN will protest that she "can't stay" even while she is taking her hat off.

IT isn't the dainty stitch in the church bazaar doily that makes smiles on papa's face, but the strong flax thread on his trousers' button.

IF a man really loves a woman he will give up smoking for her, but if she really loves him, she won't ask him to.

WE have purists and stylists who are such sticklers for exact English that they lack imagination.

Imagination is sympathy in motion. The man who has sympathy is ever a defender of the weak, a champion of the downtrodden.

We need men who express the universal language which all understand. Men who know where the berries grow, where the wild birds nest, when to sow and reap.

We need more writers who help the woman at the tub, rather than the woman at the club.

These purists usually hate wicked people. They have contempt for the unfortunate and no patience with the foolish.

OLD BILLIE from the hills says: "It seems as I come to town most of the way is up hill, and when I drive back home most of the way is up hill, too. Guess it's because the down grades are easy and don't take long."

Billie in his statement expresses the conditions in life's road. It seems up hill most of the way and we don't seem to remember the easy grades.

BRASS TACKS

THERE will be many things in Brass Tacks you have heard before; but remember old Bill Shakespeare told things over again. There is nothing new in the world. Bill's writings, and even Brass Tacks, are simply twice-told tales. It's the sauce and the new way of serving that is our excuse; and besides, there are many who haven't heard everything in Brass Tacks and maybe they'll be glad to read them. This is a big world, anyway, and if everybody stopped because of criticism there would be a sudden jar over the earth.

WHY doesn't the souvenir postal card man get up a design saying, "I've married the best man in the world." These cards would sell well at Niagara Falls and other places where honeymooners rendezvous.

WE often think we are cunning until the results come in.

THERE never was anyone so old and hardened that an alleged comic valentine didn't hurt. Don't send any. It is a snake-in-the-grass trick.

FIND out how far you are wrong yourself, and you won't be bothered greatly as to whether the old world is right or not.

YES, we find an ingrate once in awhile when we do deeds of kindness, but the gratitude offsets.

SEND those flowers today! When he's dead he can't thank you. Today he can. DO IT NOW.

THE four M's in some women's lives: Money. Matrimony. Mystery. Mastery.

IT'S a wise father who knows as much as his own son.

WHEN a woman wears an eel-fitting dress, the dress is usually symbolic of the smoothness of the wearer.

DON'T forget that "honey" will buy sweeter things than money.

"CUT that out" is a slang phrase borrowed evidently from doctors.

THE verses we see in the street car advertisement, extolling the quality of a certain brand of sausage, is, to our literary minds, merely doggerel.

*Y*OU can do what you are expected to do. You are expected to do your best, that's all.

※ ※

*W*HEN a woman with a lot of children, baskets and luggage leaves town there's no one at the depot to see her off. But when a young girl with nothing but an empty pocketbook leaves town there are enough people at the depot to start a lively Western town.

※ ※

*A*MONG the ignorant we hear talk of ghosts, hoo-doos, signs and superstitions. Luck is called the cause of success. The wise man knows that work, love, smiles, patience and hustle are the things that affect our status in life, and not the mysteries.

※ ※

*D*ON'T guy anybody. It doesn't give you much satisfaction and the one you guy will hate you. Some day you may need his friendship.

※ ※

*L*ET the wind do your sighing and the clouds weep your tears. Life is short and smiles are for us.

※ ※

*N*EXT time you are blue look in the glass and make faces at yourself.

PAPA buys his wife a sealskin, and his daughters each new dresses, for Christmas, and the family all join in and buy him a bow tie with a paste-board back and a cunning little white silk elastic loop on it to fasten it on his collar button.

P. S.—The bow tie is also charged to his account.

A FUR collar on an overcoat is no evidence of a clean undershirt.

WE do not claim any new religion. We do not claim to be the sole arbiters of right. But we are satisfied if we give any impulse or suggestion that will create sympathy which will not faint, and hope that will not falter. If we can help make the smiles chase away the frowns. If we can take your mind off that soul and body-destroying worry, we are pleased. You and we have the same feelings, aspirations and hopes. Our objective is the same. We are striving to go to the same place, and as we go hand in hand, let's cheer and help one another.

Take the notes which harmonize with yours. Forget any discord. Let's join in life's chorus and sing hallelujah for today, which is ours.

IT isn't what's on a man, but what's in him, that is the true standard of measuring him.

BRASS TACKS

A WOMAN seldom makes up her mind to do a thing. She acts on impulse and makes up her mind afterwards.

THE girl who thinks she can reform a drunkard by marrying him should grow accustomed to the washtub before she is married.

HOW lovely was her frosted wedding-cake! How stony are her biscuits!

THE question of being hard up is not any fault of the Trusts, or the National Debt, or anything of that sort. It's right down to the question of the carelessness of the individual.

The man hard up is always catching up, and catching up is a hard road to travel. If you have the gizzard to pinch expenses close for six months, and not bite off more than you can chew, you will get square and feel prosperous.

IT'S usually true that the man with very long hair is generally short on something else.

WHEN you are tired, blue and out of sorts, go to a good musical concert or play the piano.

WHEN two young men meet, they say, "What are you doing now?" Two old men meeting, "How's your health?"

LOVE is a game in which both players bluff and cheat.

A CERTAIN milkman got so drunk that he distributed cream to his patrons instead of milk. Now he's on the water wagon.

WE all have troubles and burdens to bear, but smiles help us bear them, while brooding adds to our burdens.

Do the best you can. Help what you can, and what you can't help, learn to endure philosophically.

THROW rocks at the world and the world will throw back rocks at you.

THE man who loves his wife, his children, his friends; who smiles and is kind, will make a good angel when the time comes.

AFFINITY is the worm the devil puts on his hook when fishing in the most promising whirlpool. Suckers swallow the bait without much investigation.

WE never knew a Christian Science dentist who pulled teeth with Christian Science.

"IN haste" written on the corner of an envelope makes everybody connected with the postal service get a hump. The carrier who picks up the letter runs to the postoffice. The postmaster chases to the train. The engineer on the train pulls open the throttle a little wider and the whole postal operation is jiggered up just because you put "In haste" on the envelope.

WE have just read a list of the contributions made to charity and to educational institutions for the past year. The list only included amounts of $5,000.00 and over, and the bequests ranged as high as a million and a quarter, and the total was over fifty millions of dollars.

This thing is going on every year, and it shows that the rich people are human, and kind and thoughtful.

IT is proverbial that those who have the least to worry over, worry the most.

Nervous prostration seldom comes to the six-room cottage, but often to the sixteen-room palace.

Verily, there are compensating benefits for being poor.

IF you want the thing done right and quickly, go to the busy man.

TRUTH is stone. Lies are rubber.

A LOAFER is an abomination, but a man who is busy doing foolish things is worse than a loafer.

YOUTH desires freedom from work. Mature men desire health and strength to work.

IT'S a good plan to leave an estate in the shape of life insurance policies, then you can live well on earth without trying to save every penny for your heirs. You are entitled to some of the fruits of your hand and head as well as your heirs.

A GAS METER is a machine which registers the amount of gas you are to pay for, and not, as popularly supposed, to tell the amount of gas you have used.

IF angels had to live with some men we know there would be a lot more fallen angels.

A WOMAN can keep a secret perhaps, but she can't keep the world from knowing she's keeping it.

E XPERIENCE is the compound extract of the result of butting in.

T HE cottage beats the castle as a Joy factory.

A WOMAN'S voice in song is an aeolian harp of ten thousand strings. It recalls fresh odors of the spring, the touch of mother's hand, the coo of the babe, the joy of childhood, the caress of the sweetheart.

Nothing drives away the clouds, or invades the inner recesses of the heart like that voice.

Thrice blessed is she with a voice who lives to bless, to please, to soothe, to cheer, to sympathize, to attune our hearts to the melody which uplifts us and installs within us faith, hope, charity, happiness, love and sweet content.

Thrice blessed is he whose home has a wife and mother who can and will sing as she dresses her babe and busies herself, making the home where love is the battery and life the theme.

A woman's voice is one of God's greatest gifts.

THERE are two classes in this world: Those who say "I can't" and those who say "I can."

A HIGH collar on a shipping clerk is a sure sign the clerk will never be a junior partner in the concern he's getting wages from.

TO leave your umbrella in the vestibule of the church is a sure test of Christian faith.

"MANY a girl looks sweet on the outside. So does a sugar-coated pill," says old pessimist Webb Grubb.

TODAY, before night comes, make some heart lighter by a kind word, or a smile. It costs nothing, and when your head is on the pillows tonight you'll have pleasant dreams and sound, sweet, refreshing sleep.

YES, you know it. Yet you continue to quarrel, knowing all the while that when you get angry at the other fellow, YOU are the real loser.

INSTEAD of killing the goose that lays the golden eggs it is much better to let the goose hatch out a few of the eggs, and when the young goslings grow up and begin laying golden eggs, you can then kill the old golden goose.

MONEY may turn a man's head, but a show window in a dry goods store is sure to turn a woman's head.

THE man who shoots from an ambush does it because he thinks he's safe. The man who stabs and tries to destroy through innuendo and subterfuge, does so for the same reason. What is grander, greater, and more heroic than the man who faces the world, fights in the open and calls a spade a spade.

UNTIL we see well-groomed, well-trained, well-fed children in the home of the woman's rights mother, we'll be of that old opinion still, that woman's first duty is to her family and politics comes in for second consideration.

Before woman's suffragettes can make much headway, they must have better ambassadors than old, maids, mannish women and motherless mothers.

GRIZZLY PETE says, "There's a heap more good comes from sawin' than from jawin'."

ANOTHER tradition has been blasted. Not over forty per cent of the boarding houses serve prunes.

MANY a man who has been sensible all his life lets a fool make a fool of him.

CURIOSITY is a whirlpool which has drawn many an investigator down to oblivion and perdition.

WHAT have you done today you are sorry for? Where have you hurt anyone? What opportunities have you let go by to say something that would help? How has today averaged? Did your value to yourself and to those you love go up or down by today's actions.

MANY a white vest has an empty pocketbook in it.

IT doesn't matter much whether you live up to the truth you utter. The truth helps.

Some of the best temperance truths we ever heard were given by drunkards.

If you don't feel like smiling or showing kindness, do these things anyway. The things will help the general game along.

LINCOLN said, "Let it be said of me that as I passed along life's road I always endeavored to pull the thistle and plant a rose in its place."

Lincoln knew the Today idea.

VERILY, there are two things everyone notices—dyed whiskers and painted cheeks. There never was a person in the world who could fool others with dye or paint. Knowing this, why do men dye and women paint?

MANY a woman who can't fry potatoes writes recipes for cakes to the ladies' magazines when her husband becomes famous.

You will get nearer the heart of a woman at the tub than the woman at the club.

🔨 🔨

Many a man pays two bits for a drink and tips the waiter, but never gives a newsboy a nickel and says "Keep the change."

🔨 🔨

Charity covers a multitude of sins, but mighty few sinners.

🔨 🔨

Does advanced civilization mean we commence worrying at an earlier age?

🔨 🔨

The wife caressing and flattering her husband, in order to press the advantage the opportunity offers to ask for a new gown, carries a refrain of melancholy.

🔨 🔨

Today is the tomorrow you worried about yesterday, and that dreadful thing didn't happen, did it?

🔨 🔨

"Love me and tell me so" expresses the craving in every woman's heart.

A GENTLEMAN died. The children he knew during his life chipped in their pennies and nickels and erected a monument to him. This was the epitaph: "Loving—Lovable—Loved." This is a true story.

MANY a girl who was called an angel at sixteen, looks anything but one when she is thirty-five and crosses the street in a Mother Hubbard to borrow some butter from her neighbor.

APPRECIATION is sweet. A school teacher near Frozen Dog was nearly disheartened by some big, rough, honest, but thoughtless young men in her school. One of them, the ringleader, was stricken with fever. The school teacher nursed him through his illness and saved his life. When he was strong again he said to her: "I'm all right now. I was a coyote, the way I treated you, and I want to square things up; so you just give me a list of everyone who has been mean to you and I'll start out and round 'em up and lick 'em all for you."

WE never could exactly understand why it is that a woman gets mad if other women do not admire her husband, and jealous if they do.

"IS your wife entertaining this season?" asked Grizzly Pete. "Not very," growled Webb Grubb.

SOME complaint is uttered because married men don't go into society more. There is no place in society for a married man. He got what he went there for when he got his wife.

TO keep your friend's interest, don't tell him all you know the first time you meet him. The big magazines have found that the continued story plan is the best-paying one.

THE man who usually gets the best of it in law suits, gets the worst of it outside of the courtroom.

THE meanest man we ever knew kept his wife in bed a month after she was well, so the neighbors would continue to send in good things to eat.

AS Pat says, "Half the lies about the Irish ain't true."

DIGGING for gold only brings reward to one in ten thousand; but digging for good brings rewards with every shovelful.

ONCE in a while we get tired of the hustle and the bustle and we like to walk deep into the woods, among the ferns, and rest our weary brains.

Once in a while we tire of the classical music and we like to hear old Grizzly Pete play "Old Dan Tucker" on the fiddle, or Mrs. Pete play "Home, Sweet Home" on the old melodeon.

Once in a while we tire of the cut-glass dishes and linen tablecloths and like to eat some of Aunt Emma's fried chicken on the old red damask tablecloth.

Once in a while we like to get away from the highbrows and meet our dear old, simple, honest Uncle Charlie, and sit and smoke with him in his settin' room in front of his hickory wood fire.

These once-in-awhiles are great tonics for the strenuous city man.

NO man ever went on a hunting or fishing trip without making an explanation afterward.

IT takes the hammer of practice to drive the nail of precept.

WHAT you think of yourself and what some folks think of you, is as different as the stories you tell the mercantile agency and the tax assessor.

YOUNG friend, don't marry money. You can get rid of the money all right, but you can't get rid of the trouble you get with it.

NEARLY every church has two classes among the women members. Those who are afraid the pastor will resign, and those who are afraid he won't.

TIMES have changed. To be good is no longer to be a curiosity.

AN apology doesn't wipe out the offense. It only modifies it.

"IT'S never too late to mend." That was never written by a mother of children who had to wait until the kiddies went to bed before she could fix up their clothes.

A MAN who has faithfully wound his clock every twenty-four hours for a year, and then discovers it is an eight-day clock, is justified in saying just one tiny little swear word.

THE trouble is, in feeling the public pulse, many people never let go of their own hands.

MEN who complain and men who gossip seldom have much regard for truth.

WHEN a woman really has more sense than a man, she uses some of the sense to conceal the fact from him.

COMMON sense is the powder and learning is the cap which sets it off. If the gun is loaded with a small amount of powder the effect will be small. It should be observed that the proper proportions for the loading of the gun is one hundred parts of common sense to one part of learning in order to get the best results.

LUCKY stones are found in plucky paths.

IN every fight the chances are for the stronger one winning out; the odds are never so great, however, but what there is a chance for the weaker to win; in other words, both sides have a show. But there is a fight, in which one side can never be beaten, and that is in the fight against nature. No matter how nature should see the futility of their fight and get defeated in the fight, and those who do not appreciate the value of health, but are constantly warring against nature should see the futility of their fight and get into the band wagon of health and happiness.

A DOUBLE craving is in every human heart for solitude and companionship. There are times when we long to be alone, and there are times when we long for the touch of a human hand, the glance of a human eye or a smile from human lips. Food and drink loose half their flavor when taken in solitude, but the mental pleasures are far greater when one is alone, though we should not carry companionship or solitude to the extreme. We should observe that great rule—temperance.

MANY a word spoken figuratively can be taken literally and tell the real truth. For instance, we speak of a man "following the races," and by looking in the dictionary we find "following" would indicate those left behind.

николаи one can practice cruelty and injustice without suffering. As surely as he metes out pain to others he will be repaid in bodily or mental pain, or both.

MEN resemble plants; some flower and bloom all the time and pass for good plants. The ultimate end of plants, however, is the fruit, and the men who produce results like the tree that yields much fruit are not given to flowers and beauty.

A BANK failure may not upset a depositor, but he's liable to lose his balance.

WITHOUT departing from the truth it is interesting to note the difference there is in stories told by two respectable men to a jury.

IF we eliminate conscience from our make-up we have nothing to brag of any more than a rabbit.

AN epicure is a masticator who appreciates a master caterer.

MUCH depends upon the point of view; for instance, when we tell a woman her daughter is just the image of her when she was that age the mother looks pleased but the daughter looks scared.

FOR every person that is worn out there are a hundred that have rusted out.

THE wise man is like a willow tree and the foolish man is like the hardwood tree. The willow bends and gives to the storm and comes up again smiling. The hardwood tree defies the storm and it refuses to give or bend and it is blown down. It's hard to suffer wrongs quietly. Our rebellious spirit arises at real wrongs, and fancied wrongs, but we should learn to suffer injustices once in a while, for we shall be the stronger in our position afterward. The greater a man is, the less he is disturbed by what others do or say against him unjustly. Mean natures are always at unrest. Great natures bend and suffer injustice quietly. Be right, do right, and all will be right, no matter how hard it may seem when you are abused and humiliated.

THE more one goes the round of pleasure the more difficult it is to get square.

BRASS TACKS

TRUST not the man who prefaces his remarks by saying, "I will be perfectly frank with you;" also beware of the stranger who comes to you and outlines a plan which he says is "because of his interest in you." Always remember that there is a string to every proposition.

PLACE a reasonable estimate on yourself and your abilities. Never place yourself in a cheap class unless you are cheap and wish people to know it.

DO not believe all you see, for if tombstones told the truth the horned gentleman from the warm place would have to go out of business.

THERE are two things to do when you are imposed upon, one is to stand it and the other we can't think of just at present.

DARWIN devoted much of his life to finding the missing link between man and monkey. We have found the missing link; it is nothing more or less than clothes; clothes either make a man or a monkey of the wearer.

IT'S not the work of a man that tires him. It is getting rid of bores.

AS summer rain is to the parched ground, so is a kind word of encouragement to the struggler.

A MAN who is in debt is like a cat climbing a tree—the going up is easy, but the getting back to the starting point is a long and tedious road.

IT is the roughness of the grind-stone that sharpens the ax; so it is the trouble in one's life that gives one a sharp edge.

COMMEND us to the man who does not agree with you always. You might as well go out in the timber and talk to an echo as to the person who agrees to everything you say.

WE have observed that those who can easily decide questions for their friends can seldom come to a decision in matters of their own.

BRASS TACKS

THE best way to throw dice is to throw them away.

ONE wise man can fool a dozen fools easier than a dozen fools can fool one wise man.

CONCENTRATE your energies toward making a success of one thing. If you have too many irons in the fire your specialist competitors will surely get the best of you. The way to be a specialist is to learn how to do one thing just a little better than the other fellow.

IF we show an irritable, overbearing, suspicious side of our character, we see these same things in others. We can most easily discover faults in others that we are ourselves possessed of.

IF we were more careful of where we step those who follow us would not stumble so often.

BE glad, and your friends are many. Be sad, and you lose them all. There are none to decline your nectared wine, but alone you must drink life's gall.

THERE are mushroom men and men of oak. The business that grows like a mushroom will decay and be lost sight of in a short time. The business that grows slowly like the oak, no matter how slowly if it really grows, will continue and live long like the oak. That which comes easily will go easily. The boat that's built for speed will not carry much freight. What's gained in speed is lost in power. If you want a steady paying business that will flourish after you are called away, build it up on the steady, solid oak plan. Don't bother if you see mushrooms growing on all sides. Keep everlastingly at it. Hew to the line. Move forward inch by inch, build up just a little each day. Cultivate a reputation for soundness. Be patient and you will see many generations of mushrooms born and die while you are attaining maturity.

DON'T look for mean, base motives in everyone who is trying to do something. Better get fooled once in awhile by giving a person credit for something he is not entitled to than to harm a good person by our suspicion.

NO man fully practices what he preaches, but this is no reason he shouldn't preach. The best temperance lecture we ever heard was delivered by a man under the influence of liquor.

WE hear a great deal about the iron wills of certain men. It is all right to have an iron will, but care should be taken that it is not made of pig-iron.

NEVER put off until the morrow what you can do today. Success is measured by the ability to push forward just a little each day. Success that comes in chunks is but ephemeral. Make each day average for itself. Learn to divide each day in proper proportions; get enough sleep; do enough work; take enough rest; make enough happiness for a harmonious day.

IT is a strange thing that the man who has the worst reputation is usually the one who is most afraid of having it injured.

MAKE friends with your creditors, but never make creditors of your friends.

MEN are like fish. Neither would get into trouble if they kept their mouths shut.

THE worst people in the world are the richest and the poorest.

IT is a splendid thing to hear a man voice lofty sentiments, but one single good action is better than a hundred sentiments not made use of.

THERE is one secret a man really tries to keep even from his closest friend; that is, his poverty, whether it be poverty of wealth or poverty of brains.

IT is a difficult thing for a man to keep cool when he is roasted; it is generally in the nature of things that he should get hot.

THERE is a truth about a lie and that is if you let it alone it will chase itself to death.
 The world is improving. The time is not far distant when an honest man will actually command respect.

ONE of the greatest trials we have in the world is to be compelled for business, or social reasons to listen to a man who thinks he can tell a funny story, when, as a matter of fact, he has no more idea of humor than a rabbit.

BRASS TACKS

WE cannot properly understand others unless we have something of like elements in our own natures.

GRIZZLY PETE says: "I have often wondered that the churches do not add sick benefits, life insurance, etc., as encouragement to their members. The lodges of the country have an immense membership, and this large membership is due to insurance features. When a member of a lodge is taken sick he is given every attention and receives sick benefits. When he dies his widow receives two or three thousand dollars in cash. The members of the churches pay as much as the members of the lodge, but have no insurance or guaranteed sick benefits."

IN every life there is a door marked private.

OUR faults attract more attention than our virtues.

LEARN to live one day at a time; do the best you can today, and do not worry about tomorrow.

THERE is no use wasting nice conversation on the man who won't listen to clean-cut facts.

A WELL-KNOWN man moved to New York and caught appendicitis. When he lived in Idaho he never aspired to more than chills and fever.

YOU can't avoid abuse any way you fix it. If you husband your funds to provide against poverty in your old age, people say you have no soul and money is your God. If you are a spendthrift people say you are shiftless and some day you'll be sorry.

DON'T work a good thing too hard. Don't keep cutting the wool off the sheep that lays the golden egg until you pump it dry.

WE are not discouraged. Things will right themselves. The pendulum swings one way and then the other. But the steady gravitation is toward the center of the earth. Any structure must be plumb if it is to endure or the building will fall. Wrong may seem to triumph, right may seem to be defeated. But the gravitation of eternal justice is upward.

BE a producer and source of profit to your employer and not a source of expense.

MIX with people who are successful. We are creatures of environment and we take on the qualities of those we rub against.

NO successful employer is blind to the value of employees. The men who get the valuable positions and the junior partnerships are picked out by the results they have produced and not because they kicked for advancement, or because they have bragged of their abilities. Men competent to fill high-priced positions are the scarcest. The world is still full of $10.00-a-week men. Results count and no one notices results quicker than a proprietor.

DON'T try to be a "good fellow," but be a good man. "Good fellows" at fifty are working as shipping clerks, while good men are in business for themselves at fifty.

NOTHING brings such quick returns as kindness, gentleness, cheerfulness and lending a helping hand.

PAY no attention to lies. The greater a man is, the less he is disturbed by what others do or say against him without cause.

DON'T get discouraged. The darkest hour in your career may be just before you step into the brightest hour. Changes come quickly. Moves are made rapidly on the checker-board of business. Be patient. Your time will come if you have the stuff in you. Success consists in remembering to steer clear of a mistake you have once made. Success means the ability to overcome obstacles and reverses. Success comes to those who move forward, be it ever so slowly, so long as you advance some. Hold your head up, aim high, clench your fist. Set your jaw firmly, and push forward with a determination. Let your watchword be, "I will."

IF you think twice before you speak you'll find that about ninety per cent of the time you will have no occasion to say a word.

IF you have not the force of character to make an enemy, you will never make a friend.

WE hear a great deal about the busy bee, and old Webb Grubb, the laziest man we know, remarks: "Who would not be a bee, who works three months in the summer, and loafs all winter living on honey."

BRASS TACKS

WHEN all men are what they pretend to be, jails will be torn down, churches turned into storehouses and policemen will be car drivers.

BEFORE marriage it's a case of yearning for a woman, after marriage it's a case of earning.

THERE is a certain pride in long ancestry that is enjoyable. It is nice to be able to look back upon a noble line of men and know yourself to be one of their descendants. But don't stop there. Be a man of mark yourself. In this modern democratic world it is the man, not the name that counts. The man who has nothing to boast of but his illustrious ancestry is like a potato plant—the only good belonging to him is underground.

TO be happy you must work. The most miserable people in this world are those who do not work and who live without aims or ambitions.

SOME old geezer said fine feathers made fine birds. We have noticed that fine birds are short lived, and also that they are good for nothing but their beauty.

A STITCH in time saves nine, but it don't save nine unless you take the stitch; thinking won't do it. Procrastination is the thief of business.

A YOUNG man still in the early thirties, though a power in the business world, got his first position, one of office boy, in the following manner. He entered a business man's office the afternoon of the day he quit school. "I'm in a hurry, if you please," he said to the man who paid no attention to him, though he had been in the room a minute. "What do you want?" asked the man deliberately, looking up from his paper. "I want a job as office boy," he answered. "Well, what are you in such a hurry about?" queried the man, somewhat astonished. "Because I've been out of school two hours now and haven't got a job yet. If you haven't got a job for me, why say so, and I'll move along, as I haven't any time to lose." "I guess I need one of your kind," said the man, "you may stay."

THE devil gets in great work when the time comes around to schedule personal property.

IT'S all right to be rich, if you can manage not to appear so.

THE man with little money is frequently more generous than the man of wealth, because he does not wish others to think he has but little.

IF a crowd of women go out together in the evening, they have soda water, peanuts, chocolate creams, and a lunch after they get to their destination, all of which enables the physician to put rubber tires on their broughams.

SOME men divide their time equally—one-half making promises, one-half making excuses. If you make no promises you'll need no excuses, and can then devote ALL your time to getting business.

IT'S better to be over-cautious than over-credulous.

THERE'S many a good thing lost by not asking for it.

IF your work worries you it is evidence your position is a little larger than you are. Therefore, strive to grow until you fit your place.

WHEN writing or speaking use plain, pointed words, and above all steer away from words of double or doubtful meaning.

UNDERTAKERS report that they never saw a death certificate that read "killed by kindness."

REMEMBER that when a man gives his reason for anything, that it is quite likely the reason is pretended, not real.

PUT not your trust in a gold mine, an effusive friend, or a slanderer.

WHENEVER you have a favor conferred on you, remember it; but when you do a favor, forget it. The practice of this truth is one of the things that go toward building a great character.

MOST men look through their I's, but they see themselves only.

YOU can neither make a good knife out of bad steel, nor a good business—out of bad schemes.

WE have often remarked that there's a string to every proposition. There are no snares so dangerous as those that are laid for us under the name of good offices.

SINCE time began the ten fingers of a man have been his best friends.

MANSLAUGHTER is a penal offense. Man's laughter isn't. Spelled the same.

IF there is anything in the theory of the survival of the fittest, a lot of people we know must have been overlooked.

IT is not always the squarest men that move in the best circles.

'TIS not so much how much you say, 'tis how you say what you say.

MANY a youth who aspires to become an A. M. is in after years glad to settle down as the village P. M.

IT is a great mistake to hire old friends to work for you. It is difficult to force obedience from those with whom one has birdnested.

❧ ❧

AN employe of a railroad got $1,000 for writing three words for railroad crossing signs. These words were: Stop! Look! Listen!

❧ ❧

PASTE this in your memorandum book, and whenever you have that worried feeling look at it, for it is one of the greatest truths we have ever known: Nine-tenths of the worry in this world comes from anticipating supposed troubles that never occur.

❧ ❧

A STRANGE paradox: A woman never becomes a new woman until she is an old woman.

❧ ❧

CONSTANT craving for company and the horror of being alone is a sign of mental weakness. Man grows in solitude. Good business plans, good ideas, are always worked out in solitude. Take an hour or two each day by yourself and think.

THE man who persists in doing others, often terminates his career by doing time.

IF you have a poor memory you can cure yourself by lending small sums to your friends.

LINGUISTS tell us that there is no such word as worry in the language of the savage.

THE man who is ever suspicious of others and ever ready to say ill of other men cannot be happy. The seed that is sown is the seed that will be harvested. You can't have friends if you spend your time making enemies.

THE hardest thing for a woman to decide is when to commence her thirtieth year.

THERE'S always hope for the man who works, but despair for the fellow who waits for something to turn up.

A MAN can't make love successfully if there is a cuckoo clock in the room.

IT is a good thing to remember funny stories. When you feel blue, angry or worried, hunt up some round-faced, stout man who enjoys a good laugh, and tell him a funny story; it will cure you to see him laugh.

CENTURIES ago the great philosopher, Confucius, walking through a forest when a common Chinaman stopped him and said: "Oh, great man, we poor creatures of the earth hear much of thy learning and of thy religion. Thou speakest much we do not understand, and more than we fain can remember. 'Mongst us poor common people is much discussion as to thy teaching, for each hath but a fragment of thine understandings, and we cannot make a complete fitting of thy great words. Do us, therefore, the great favor to tell us how to live, and make thy discourse only so long as I shall be be able to stand upon one foot, for that much only can my small understanding and my poor brain remember." Whereupon the great man said: "I will give thee the essence of all the truth I teach. Stand thou therefore upon thy foot." And he said to the poor man, "Do unto others as you would have them do unto you."

DON'T think because a man has done you a favor he is under everlasting obligations to you.

THE normal condition of man is that of happiness. Worry is the result of an artificial condition.

ONE string out of tune will spoil the music played on the best piano. The false note is more marked than all the good ones. It creates a discord. A man who lives in harmony has discovered the secret of life. He is in perfect tune. If a man occupies his time and mind with harmony he does not get angry and does not worry. You are not angry at this moment because you are thinking better things. Make each successive while like the present moment and discord will die out, and your friends won't hear these notes that grate on the ear.

THE good business man does nothing in a hurry. He employs no one to do what he can't do himself. He keeps his engagements. He keeps his designs and business secrets to himself. He considers justice in his dealings with others. He is clear and explicit in making bargains. He takes pleasure in his business.

THERE is no man suddenly good or evil. The process is gradual.

THE optimist makes his own heaven, and enjoys it as he goes through life. The pessimist makes his own hell and suffers it as he goes through life.

WHEN there is a ghost of a chance never give up until you give up the ghost.

NO man can dictate to another his belief, nor assume that he is the sole observer of truth.

THE ability to say no is more valuable to a man than the ability to read Latin.

THE more we accustom ourselves to the truth the surer we are in detecting the ring of truth in others, the more we lie the more we believe others are lying.

ONE ungrateful man does an injury to all who stand in need of aid.

FRIENDSHIP is a strong and habitual inclination in two persons to furnish the good and happiness of each other.

THERE was never a person who loved his fellow man and also loved riches.

THERE is no better mark of sterling character than the moral independence that forgoes a popular pleasure for duty's sake—that refuses to "go with the crowd" —and such a character will eventually cause the crowd to come its way.

TIMES change: several years ago the business man took his pen in hand and now some of them take their typewriter in arms.

A GOOD memory is a valuable thing, but it is also well if you have a good forgetory.

MEN and pins are useless when they lose their heads.

A MAN that is bright will pause to reflect instead of jumping at a conclusion.

※ ※

MOST men seem to have two objects in life: one is to become rich and the other is to become richer.

※ ※

A MAN who does the square thing always is like the man with a clean undershirt. He may be misjudged, but finally the truth will be known, and it will shine forth the stronger, because unexpected.

※ ※

THE darkest hour is just before dawn; if you don't believe it ask a man who has "made a night of it."

※ ※

WHEN a man tries to drown his troubles it seems that he thinks that his trouble is in his stomach.

※ ※

THE easiest time to deceive a man is when he is trying to deceive you.

※ ※

A MAN is never as good as he says he is or as bad as others say he is.

BRASS TACKS

UNLESS I get some happiness every day now, I will never be able to find it on any tomorrow.

The thought that these lines may build up hope and cause some brother to resolve to get the happiness habit makes us happy. We have tried all kinds of plans, but happiness is the greatest treasure we ever possessed and we would not trade the happiness we have had and are having every day for all the money in the world without happiness. Every day is worth a thousand dollars to us from our standpoint.

CLEANLINESS, exercise, fresh air, a regular vocation, prudent conduct and home love produce good living, and indolence, shiftlessness, dishonesty, suspicion and malice make life miserable and destroy it.

THERE is no substitute for rest. Medicine is a makeshift. Braces and tonics are temporary. Get plenty of sleep, spend more evenings at home, surrounded by quiet influences. The man who works hard all day and seeks excitement in the evening soon finds "there's something wrong" and he is lagging behind in the procession. He gets a cheaper job and is a has-been. The young man who passes him at the half-mile post is the man who takes rest and takes care of his health.

RISE up each morning and the first thing you do resolve to be good humored until about ten o'clock—the rest of the day will take care of itself. Crossness and unkind words are the ground glass in the bearings of a machine—they hurt the working.

HEALTH is a property and the property, like any other property, improves or runs down accordingly as it is cared for. Health is the most valuable property in the world and should have much of every man's attention. The possession of good health helps you in your business. Poor health and good business don't make a good pair.

REMEMBER that the scarcity of work is not in it, compared with the scarcity of good men.

ALL good work begins with contentment. The heart must sing while the hand toils, if good work is to be achieved.

EMERGENCY to the real man is simply opportunity. The more frequently we overcome obstacles, the easier the overcoming.

GOOD manners will tend to make any man attractive.

WHEN a man's own dog won't follow him beware of that man.

SOME sigh for a life of pampered ease and perfumed luxury in a silken nest. But no man can be happy unless he works for that which he has.

PEOPLE who are in the shadowland of tears and sorrow, welcome a laugh and a hearty handshake. The smile and the rainbow whisper of hope.

WHEN a woman is looking for her lover she sees someone on every street corner who resembles him. He is so constantly and persistently in her mind that every passer-by takes on his semblance. The man who has bad motives and a sour stomach looks for bad motives, as the basis of every act in others. The man with a mean disposition shows it in his face and he reflects himself in every one else. The man with a smile, the man wth the cheery good morning, with the warm hand-shake, with the sympathetic soul, sees happiness and joy and smiling faces all about him, and he enjoys his life. The side of life we see is the side we show.

WE are prone to pander to the things we like to do. A perfect physique is only obtained by building up the weaker parts. We must learn to do things we do not like to do if we expect to get on in the world.

BEWARE of the man who does not like children, dogs, music and laughter.

MANY a man has won success with the captivating smile and the glad hand.

MANY a kid glove conceals the hand of steel, likewise many a kid glove conceals the hand of steal; therefore never judge by external appearances.

A HEN trying to steal a nest does not act more suspiciously than an old girl preparing for her wedding while trying to keep it a secret.

WHEN the room is too dark for rubber plants, or a nursery, the wife always furnishes it with things she don't know what to do with and calls it a "den."

MANY a woman passes for a beauty because people have never seen her with her head soaked, ready for a washing.

A SUICIDE is one person who has had his own way, but he does not look any happier for it.

NEXT time you get real good and angry, go to the looking glass.

IF you want to make a hit with your friend's wife, as well as your friend, tell the wife how nicely she has made her old dress over, in the presence of her husband.

IN the old days, a walk down the lane and a couple of red apples was the thing. In the new days, it's a ride in a carriage and a couple of red lobsters.

THERE are four ways we love a girl: For her self, for her wealth, for her social standing, and because we can't help it.

IF we would think less about Siberia and Kongo, and think more about some of our Southern convict camps, we would understand more about the glass house and stone throwing business.

※ ※

IF you are going to build a house, you put the figures down in black and white. If you want to know where you stand financially, you put down your debits and credits on a piece of paper. Next time you feel blue and are worried, take a sheet of paper and put down the good things in one column, and your fancied burdens in the other. Head the good or credit side with Love, Health and the fact that you are alive. After you have filled up both columns, you will find the credit side is real, and the debit side largely imagination. The schedule will surprise you.

※ ※

WE once knew a girl who graduated in a Boston musical conservatory, and when she returned to her home still remembered and still would play the old songs and things her friends wanted to hear.

※ ※

THE divorce courts show very few divorces asked for by the parents who have over three children.

EVERY man inherits one of the three B's: Brains, Birth, or Boodle; and we wish to go on record that when the young men call at our house to pay courtship to our daughters, the young men with Brains will find the daughters' papa will be less severe with them than with the Birth and Boodle fellows.

SOME day when you feel blue and down on your luck, visit a hospital and talk with a few of the patients and see how nobly they bear their real troubles, and how cowardly you bear your fancied troubles.

THE young doctor calls diseases by their Latin names, but the old doctor calls them by the regular old-fashioned names.

CROSS your heart—did you ever admire a woman who was a big light in a literary club?

WE have just returned from a visit to our natal town, and that "old swimmin' hole" is a frog pond; and "things don't look like they used to was." The things haven't changed, but we have.

SOME bright man will establish a "Work Cure" for brain-tired people, and it will give the "Rest Cures" the hottest kind of competition.

People worry and fret and stew until they get a case of "Willies"; then they go to a Rest Cure and get worse.

The thing is, work with the hands when the head is tired, and that will rest the brain.

THE hand, the heart and the head form a triangle that can bring untold happiness, if used together. One alone is not much service, any more than one blade of a scissors.

FIGURES don't lie excepting when connected with a woman's age, or a man's between 41 and 63.

THE illumination of the sun, and less of the double-ended candle, is better for us.

"GENERALLY speaking," says Grizzly Pete, "prize-fighters and preachers go where they hang up the biggest purse."

BRASS TACKS

THE schoolmarm at Frozen Dog says the male sex consists of men, lovers and husbands.

WHY is it, sisters, that when you get past the "fair, fat and forty" period, you complain that the millinery styles are not as becoming as they used to be?

THE boy who was raised near the grass roots is the big man of the city.

SINCE the automobiles have come, the recorder's office shows a great increase in mortgages.

LABOR is health. Idleness saps the powers of aspiration, attempt and achievement, and causes them to atrophy and rot.

OPTIMISM is life—Pessimism, slow suicide.

MISERY loves company, but remember it loves cheerful company.

ANGER wrecks nerves and later becomes a chronic disease.

WE men struggle for something for the inner man. Women struggle for something for the outer woman.

PAT KELLY apologized to Grizzly Pete for abusing him the day before. Pete replied: "Some mistake, Pat; I didn't see you yesterday." Pat smoked a minute, then said: "I have it now; I dreamed that row."

YES, man has one advantage. He can get married if he wants to.

ART thou weary and tired? Hast thou dread of impending evil? Dost thou feel thy friends have forsaken thee? Dost the clouds obscure the sun? Is the future blank?

Dear one, it's worry that's eating thee. That dreadful thing won't happen. Get this in thy gizzard. It's good stuff. Live today. Put the past behind thee. The future hasn't happened and there never will be any future.